I'd like you to meet the unknown grand-daughter of Man O' War, the greatest race horse in U.S. history.

Two young, pretty girls, an unforgettable summer and a magnificent horse. Set in the late 50's when all the rage was Elvis. Switch blades and bobby socks. Country life was a whole other matter.

This is a story of the greatest summer of my life, the greatest of friendships and the love of a wonderful horse.

I am ready to tell the story. I'm 61 now, and have told this story many times, to my children. Those children want me to share this story with the world.

This book is about the personal experiences with the unknown grand-daughter of Man O War, the greatest race horse in U.S. history. She was never known or raced because no-one expected her to live through a serious bout with pneumonia, when she was just 3 months old.

As a result of this illness, she wound up nothing more than a family pet. A pitiful waste of magnificent horse flesh, as she clocked at over 38 mph and continuously maintained that speed for lengths of over 3 miles. Had she ever been trained and raced, I believe she would have stepped gracefully into her grand-father's footsteps in history.

I knew the family who brought her home and nursed her to health. Her life, although pleasant for the first few years, took a turn when she was about 4 years old, which ruined her health but then later rescued. A family pet, her name was simply 'Winnie'.

The book revolves around the lives of two young girls but the heart is 'Winnie's' untold story

Chapter 1

Thirteen years old and ripped up from a known world, and then brought into an unknown world called 'country'. An undiscovered world lay before me. My life was about to change forever.

I stood on the front lawn, near the road, watching my father and a friend, lift the couch into our new home. I wasn't quite sure why we had moved to the valley, but then my parents were always moving. 'The Valley', that's all people called it.

The truth is there are two valleys in Albuquerque: the north valley, and the south valley. Both were outside the city district, back in those days. The south valley is more of a farming community, while the north valley is more like a country community.

In that region, the Rio Grande River runs north and south. Along both sides, several miles away, there is a mountain range to the east and a high bluff ridge to the west. Rain and snow melt off, from both sides, runs down toward the river, which makes the valley area rich soil.

This was long before the city put in a flood control system. We still lived with the deadly floods, especially near the arroyos. An arroyo is a wash, where the flooding rains flow down from higher ground. Coming down from the mountains, the arroyos could flow as deep as 20 feet and at speeds that were deadly.

After centuries of flooding rains, many arroyos had widened as much as 20 feet, with banks that dropped off sharply, as deep as 6 feet. This was certainly no place to be walking, when the roaring flood came pounding down the 10-mile stretch from the foothills, to the river.

From higher ground, the valley looks like a thick green oasis, running the length of the river, all the way through the state. Being outside the city limits, this part of the valley was unique in that back yards were horse corrals, and animal pens. Small patches of neighborhood mingled with small croplands.

Across the street, from where we were moving in, there was a back yard filled with chickens. A small irrigation ditch ran the length of the block, along behind the houses. Folks still burned their own trash in barrels, out by the irrigation ditch.

A little farther to the north is an area called 'Alameda', which means (from the old days) 'look at the trees'. Cottonwood trees dominate the whole territory. Some of these trees are over 100 years old and stand 3 and 4 stories high.

This was, and still is today, country to the bone. It's a relaxed atmosphere where kids run free. There are so many adventures the children are never bored.

This was New Mexico. These days, homes look like mansions compared to what the norm was, in the 50's. Most average homes followed the theme of the adobe. The adobe home looks somewhat like a mud box, to most anyone who didn't live in pueblo country. Every corner is rounded off and wood framing around the windows have an Aztec pattern. For the most part, the colors are beige and browns. Ceilings consist of huge, dark stained logs, exposed to view. The logs continue throughout the building, extending through the outer walls, sticking out several inches outside. These logs are called vigas.

Exterior decorations consist of things like clay sun faces from Mexico and chili ristras, which are chili peppers strung together. Traditionally, the chilies are strung together, and hung outside the front or back door, to dry. Fresh air is the best way to dry peppers.

This new neighborhood consisted of all the old and traditional ways of the pueblo region. Most of the homes were built just after WWII, old but quaint and groomed. The back yards were enormous, as most folks still had their own vegetable gardens, along with a few farm animals.

The house, we now called home, was tiny compared to today's standards. There were only 3 bedrooms. With three children, ages 13, 11 and 7, this little house was a cramp.

For the first time in years, I would have to share my bedroom with my little sister. What's more, I had to share my double bed. I wasn't happy about that situation but, I was just a kid and hardly had a say.

Numerous dramas were coming my way. Sometimes it's a good thing, we can't see into the future.

Chapter 2

As I eyed the neighborhood, wondering about the people, a young girl road up on a black horse, and wearing a light weight jacket. This being March, it wasn't quite spring and not quite winter. One would have to call it almost cold, just sweater weather but the sun was shining and we had a slight breeze.

I will never quite be able to explain or even put my finger on it, but there was something regal in this girl's appearance and mannerisms. Something about this girl made me want to know her better. This was a future friend.

Like me, she wore pedal pushers and tennis shoes. She had sandy colored hair, with long soft curls, that hung just below her shoulders, all wind tossed from riding. She was also about the same size as me, about 5'4" and 115 pounds or so. The difference between us was her frailty. I was one of those sturdy tomboys.

My mother had just recently cut my hair so short; it fell into a natural ducktail. My fiery red hair was a sharp contrast to that of this girl.

"Hi", she said, "You moving in?"
"Yup."
"My name is Charlotte but everybody calls me Willie, because my middle name is Willow. Charlotte Willow. How old are you"?
"I'm 13. And you?" I asked.

"Me too. You'll probably be checking into the school, in the morning."

"Yeah. What's it like?", I asked.

Willie filled me in about the school and we chatted for a while. I asked her if the school offered chorus. She was delighted to find out that I, too, sang.

"What part do *you* sing?" she asked.

"I'm alto." I told her.

"Fantastic! I'm soprano. We can practice, together. I know some great rounders, I'll teach you."

Then she asked, "You like horses?", and I replied, "Oh, most definitely!"

"Can you go for a ride? I'll show you the neighborhood".

I ran to ask my mother, "Mother. There's a girl outside that wants me to go riding her horse, with her. She wants to show me the neighborhood."

Thank goodness, mom was in a good mood or maybe she was just too busy to think about it. She simply said, "I guess so. You're sure not going to be of any help around here."

With that, we were off, riding double, to see my new surroundings. Willie was grateful to find a new friend and told me how great it was going to be, having someone to walk home with, after school. I was grateful to have a new friend to show me the ropes.

The street dead-ended just beyond our new home. Beyond the end of the street, there was a field of weeds and grass. The small irrigation ditch that ran along behind my house extended beyond the houses and all the way through the field. We rode along the ditch and out through the field where I was to discover the railroad tracks. I never needed an alarm clock, as the train went by just before 6 AM, every morning, and blew its horn.

She introduced me to the old Cottonwood tree with the hollow trunk. She explained that it had been hit by lightning several times. It stood in a whole row of huge trees that had grown along the banks of the tiny irrigation ditch. One can only imagine why this one tree, among all the others, was the only one hit by lightning and so many times.

At the other end of my street, was highway 47, 2nd street to us. The next block over, Willie rode along the side of the irrigation ditch, which ran between the backyards, and pointed out Mary's house. Mary was another student our age, going to the same school I would attend. Nancy's house was two doors down from me, the last house at the dead end.

Down the street, halfway between Willie's house and mine, and across the street, there was a man who owned pure wolves, penned up in the back yard. Willie told me that not long before I came along, one of those wolves got out and attacked a small child.

After riding up and down each street, in the neighborhood, she stopped by her house to introduce me to her mother.

Willie's mom was like no one I had ever met before.

About 50 years old, she wore her strawberry blonde hair pulled tightly back into a small bun. Although she wore jeans, she had an air about her that I can only describe as 'prissy and stern'. Oddly enough, this woman was hardly stern, but she gave off that impression.

Their home was very different from my own. There were hardwood floors and very simplistic furniture. Something about the house and the people living in it, made one talk in hushed tones. I never quite understood why. They seemed normal enough but very reserved and very quiet. I could see where Willie got her short-stepped walk, as though afraid to lose control of her actions.

In Willie's presence, I always had the feeling I was the bull in the china shop. How very different these people were from my own family.

In my house there were three very boisterous children: little brother, my even younger sister, and myself (the eldest). Compared to this family, we were nothing but loud.

Willie was a fragile thing. Her mother told me that she was born with a hole in her back, and if not for surgery would not have lived. I soon became Willie's protector. How we became such inseparable friends, I will never really know because Willie was about as opposite from myself as one can get.

Scanned Old Photo of Judy(left)and Willie(right

Chapter 3

Riding the horse after school, each day, became the routine for Willie and I. It was not long before I noticed yet another horse out behind her house.

"Hey, Willie! Whose horse is that one?" I asked.
"Oh that's Winnie. She belongs to my sister, Charlotte".
I thought, "Two Charlotte's in the same family? Is that odd or what?" So this was, for some reason, why they called her Willie, while the older sister they called Charlotte. I never asked and certainly never found out the whole story about the names of these two girls. I just took it for what it was, and let it go at that.

I went with Willie to unsaddle the horse and brush him down. While we were tending to him, I kept noticing the other horse still in the pen, shoving against the gate, as though wanting to come out. I felt so sorry for her. So far, I had not seen anybody pay attention to her, groom her or even take her out on a ride.

I honestly could not understand how anybody could ignore such a beautiful horse. She had a magnetic spirit and wonderful form. A brown and white paint, she had reddish brown patches on her rump, the side of her neck and her underbelly. She was marvelous to behold.

This was one high-headed horse with spirit to spare. She had a huge barrel torso that narrowed down to tiny looking tummy. The vision of her chest was mesmerizing. The muscles seemed immense with distinguishable lines. Her walk was straight and strong. I saw such power in those legs and so wanted to see them running.

I could see hints of thoroughbred, with the hindquarters of the quarter horse. What might she be like to race?

I had this natural talent for picking out the winners at the racetrack. My mother once took me along. I stood on the sidelines, watching the horses warm up. Just watching the mannerisms, the sparkle in the eyes, the body length and position of the legs, I chose the winner and the runner up.

Mother decided to test my assumptions and placed bets according to what I told her. I had chosen wrong. The one I chose to win was the runner up and the one I chose to come in second, actually won the race. Twice, we went through this routine. On the third try, mother reversed what I said and would you believe, this time I was right.

By now, mother was fit to be tied. She was getting so frustrated with me. We did discover, however, that I had a talent for simply, naturally picking out horses.

Now, here I stood looking at the fastest body, I had ever seen and wondering if I would ever get to see her run.

I had an overwhelming desire to climb into that paddock and brush the other horse but Willie said, "No. You don't want to mess with that one." I left it alone. I was not that familiar with the family yet, and did not want to step on toes.

Willie's horse was a gelding. A Tennessee Walker, and an old retired roping horse. His demeanor was that of a loving old friend and his name was Starlight. Starlight stood about 15 hands high, and for his age was fit. Such a gentle soul he was, and tolerated a lot of shenanigans out of two silly girls.

For those who don't know, 15 hands is about the average size of a full-grown horse. 'Sixteen hands' would be considered large.

We often would take him out to ride bareback and double, wearing shorts and going bare foot. The only problem with riding Starlight bareback was the fact that he was old and his spine was like riding a wooden fence. For that reason, we rarely went any faster than a walk but then there were those times when we got rambunctious. From a nice stride of gallop, when we decided it was time to slow back to a walk, we both knew what we were in for.

Slowing from a gallop, down to a trot and then a walk, the ride became brutal. We clinched our thighs together, in self-defense, which caused us both to lose grip on his belly. As a result, by the time Starlight was stopped, Willie was astraddle his ears and I had bounced all the way up passed his withers. What a funny sight, we must have been. How dumb can two girls get to be putting themselves through this repeatedly? Who can explain youth?

The funniest part is the fact that even Starlight seemed to know what was about to happen. He lowered his head, just as he stopped, in preparation for 100 pounds of young girl to come sliding up to his ears. Since Willie was always in front, she just walked off the front of his head, came around and remounted.

Along 2nd street, there is a ditch. Folks referred to it as the 'clear ditch'. It is the main irrigation though out the north valley area. This ditch is close to 20 feet across and at least 15 feet deep, wide at the top and narrow at the bottom. Between the ditch and the highway, which run parallel, is a wide patch of dirt about 30 feet wide and that is the favored horse-riding path. Willie and I spent most of our time, riding along the highway on this patch of dirt.

At that time, 2nd street was the main truck route running north and south through the city. It was common to hear the trucker's air horns, as they blasted away at the pretty girls riding horses, along the highway.

When we were not riding along the highway, we were riding the other direction from my house. We would go past the end of our street, across the grassy field and wander along the railroad track.

As the train would pass by, the engineer waved at us, sometimes blowing silly kisses our way. This became such a routine, that one day he threw out a huge bag of hard candy, for us. The bag broke and we spent an hour gathering it all up. Now that was fun. A week later, he did it again.

Willie taught me new songs that we sang along the trail, everywhere we went. My favorite, we called "I love the rolling hills". I have no idea what the song's real name is. It went like this:

I love the mountains, I love the rolling hills.
I love the flowers, I love the daffodils.
I love the fires glow, when all the lights are low.
Boom-di-ada. Boom-di-ada. Boom-di-ada. Boom-di-ada.

It was a rounder song. While one sang the verse, the other sang the chorus of boom-di-ada. Just a sweet song that meant nothing but we loved it. Everywhere we rode, we sang. We were both doing the things we loved the most: riding horses and singing.

The horses both seemed to love our singing. You can tell what a horse is paying attention to, by watching their ears. For the most part, when out on a walk, those ears are forward because they're watching where they are walking. Little noises spook them, and they are constantly listening to their surroundings. You will see an ear dash off to one side and then back to the front. When the rider is verbalizing a command, the ears will go back, to listen. Watch out when those ears go back and flatten against the head. It means only one thing. They are about to get rid of the rider.

When Willie and I sang, those ears constantly moved from front to back; back and forth, back and forth.

When Willie's older sister Charlotte, disappeared from the scene, I asked her about her sister. I had no idea that Charlotte was old enough to marry but that's exactly what happened. Charlotte had married and moved off to her own home.

My curiosity perked as I realized the mysterious horse, in Willie's back yard, belonged to Charlotte. "What about Charlotte's horse? Is she going to take her?" All I got for an answer was, "I doubt it".

JUNE 1960

This is me, at the age of 14, sitting on Starlight.

Chapter 4

A few days later, as Willie and I walked home from school, I began asking again, about her sister's horse. "Does she ever ride her?" I asked.

"No, not any more. She's more interested in boys and being a teenager, to care about Winnie, any more."

"Well, why don't we take her out? Would she care?" It seemed such a waste to leave any animal just standing around all day, every day. Especially when it was obvious, the horse was bored out of its mind, and wanted to go.

Willie stopped walking, took on a serious frown and said, "You don't know what you're asking. That's a crazy horse."

"What? Crazy? She looks fine to me!" I chirped back, giving her a look that said "You're nuts".

Willie then explained to me who Winnie was and where she came from. " You ever hear of Man O' War?"

"Yeah."

"Well, Winnie is the grand-daughter of Man O' War. She has his same temperament but this isn't a racetrack and we hardly have the facilities to accommodate a crazy racing attitude. "

Rumor had it that Man O'War had a strange temperament. According to the stories handed down, he couldn't stand to see another horse ahead of him. He would bust his heart, before he would let any other horse stay out ahead and just had to pass into the lead.

I began talking before what she had said, truly sunk in. "But Willie…….I can't stand seeing her …..Wait a sec! Man O' War? How is that possible? Winnie is a paint! She has more quarter horse in her than any possible thoroughbred blood. How does that happen?"
"I didn't say she was sanctioned. Just that she was his blood. But she *is* his granddaughter. If not for illness, when she was born, she'd have the papers to prove it."
"Illness?" Now I was more curious than ever.

Willie explained, "My folks are friends of the breeder. They happened to go see him when they decided to get a horse for Charlotte. That's when they witnessed this poor little filly, dying of pneumonia. The breeder was going to put her down but my parents told him they wanted her. So he sold Winnie to us for $30, as is. Nobody expected her to make it. She was only 3 months old and suffering with pneumonia and just about dead. We didn't want to see her die, so we decided to fight for her and try to save her. And guess what? She made it!"

Willie's story about how Winnie was nursed back to health was almost riveting. The family spent day and night, rubbing her down and tending to her medicine, keeping her warm and hand feeding her. According to Willie, it took almost 3 months of her short life, to overcome this devastating condition. To look at her now, you'd never guess she had such a feeble start in life. I couldn't even draw a picture in my mind, of this frail little filly, after having seen Winnie all grown up.

I just stared, like a bumbling fool and finally said, "Well......" Charlotte was reading my mind and said, "No papers. The reason being, keeping the bloodline clean and the breeder didn't think she would ever be strong enough to continue the bloodline. That was the deal. If we wanted her, we could take her but without papers. So...well....that's that!"

"Wow", I thought. The bloodline of Man O' War and no papers..... All I could do was blink. This was mind-blowing news.

That still didn't explain why we couldn't take the horse out and let her see the world. From my point of view, Willie was just a wilting flower, afraid of her own shadow. What could be so crazy about riding a horse?

Race enthusiasts consider Man O'War to be the greatest racehorse who ever lived, winning 20 out of 21 races. He was born to race. After having seen Winnie, it all made sense. This too, seemed to be a horse born to run. Considering her situation, she would never be tested.

Chapter 5

Life at home was no bed of roses. It's no wonder I spent my days riding off with Willie. Money was tight.

The Chorus teacher told us we would have to have a white blouse and black skirt with black shoes. We had a concert coming up soon. When I asked my mother, she said, "We can't afford it" and my heart sank. Somehow, and just in time, she came through with the clothes but I was so tired of hearing that, "We can't afford it".

For some odd reason, my baby sister was going through a stage of throwing up, all the time. Sharing a bed with her was certainly no fun. One night, a few minutes after she had fallen asleep, she suddenly rose up, leaned over my pillow and threw up. Why me?

My grandparents came, from south Texas, for a visit. On grandmother's insistence, she did not want to put the children out of their beds, she and grandpa slept on cots out in the carport.

That's the way things were done, back in those days. Visiting family didn't go to a motel. Family took care of family and put them up, in their homes. We just made room for more.

The carport consisted of three solid walls but was open in the front. They put up a huge curtain across the front, to make a room. It's a good thing the weather was warm. I felt guilty, the whole time they were there and would have gladly given up my bedroom for them.

As if that wasn't bad enough, my aunt came to visit, uninvited, along with her husband and new baby. There was no love loss between my aunt and I, as this was the girl who had abused me when I was just a year old.

Betty was only about 13, at the time. She, being my mother's little sister, was always jealous of my mother. When my mother married, it aggravated my aunt. For the first time, my mother had something that Betty could not take from her. When I came along, Betty took it out on me, in secret. It was something only she and I knew because, at the time, I was only a year old.

Needless to say, I hated my aunt. Now she was in my living room, pushing her way into an already crowded situation.

Mother made us two girls, give up the bedroom and let my aunt and uncle, along with their baby, take over. During their stay, their baby chewed the nose off my favorite Teddy Bear.

Their second day visiting, I came home from school, expecting to change my clothes and go riding with Willie, as usual. As I came through the front door, my aunt said, "Judy. Would you mind taking the baby for a walk?" This meant pushing a stroller around the block.

Considering that my aunt never lifted a finger to help with anything, whenever she came to visit, I saw no reason why I should have to tend to her motherly duties. I said, "No", which was promptly followed by my mother's voice demanding, "You can help your aunt out. Take the baby for a walk!"

I was forced to call Willie, to let her know that I was unavailable to go riding, today. Making a simple phone call, back in those days, was no fun either. We had, what was called, a 'party line', which meant we could have up to five other homes using the same line. The only way we knew which incoming calls were for whom, was by the number of rings: one long ring, one short ring, two short rings or one long and one short ring. Youngsters today just don't know what they are missing.

Willie, gracefully came along for the walk, bless her heart. As girls will do, I unloaded my bitter feelings toward my aunt. Willie was a great friend and tried to make suggestions that might help.

The next day, I came home from school to hear the same commands. Knowing that my aunt was doing this to me, for the same reasons as always, this was the day of the great explosion. I flatly refused. When my mother again insisted, I again refused.

I wound up in my mother's bedroom, her finger in my face and demanding for me to be kind to her sister. For the first time in my life, I came against my mother and flatly refused. Before long, emotions flared and I uttered the words, I had held back for over 12 years. "I don't give a damn about her. I hope she dies!"

This, of course, rocked my mother's world. I had never before, denied my mother anything. I had never expressed my hatred toward anybody, much less her own sister. I did not take that baby for a walk. I did go riding with Willie.

The great divide, between my mother and me, began that very day. She never knew what her sister had done to me. I never told her. From a child's point of view, I saw my mother siding with my enemy.

Chapter 6

Life was not all horses and Willie. I spent hours, playing with my little sister. She was small enough to ride on my back, while I got on all fours and pretended to be her horse. We trotted all over the front yard, all over the house. I was my baby sister's delight.

My brother, on the other hand, was a rip-snort. He brought two of his little friends into the house, one day, just to ask my mother, "Tell them about when Judy used to wash her hair, in the toilet".
My mother replied, "It was about the same age as when you used to eat, what you did in your diapers". I laughed so hard, my face was wet with tears.

School was a whole other world. A world, I certainly was not used to. I had entered the world of switchblades and fights, jealousy and opposing gangs.

As it turned out, Willie and I didn't share one class. Even for chorus, she had it an hour before me. At least, we had each other for company on the walk to and from school.

Behind the school, and still on the school property, there was a small stable with three compartments, for the student's horses. On occasion, Willie and I rode Starlight to school. We would bring along, a fold of hay, to keep him occupied.

I had no idea, that the ringleader of the local gang had an immediate crush on me. As I later discovered, this was the reason several of the girls constantly tormented me. The school laid out in several long buildings, with six classrooms in each. The students were constantly passing from building to building, going to their next class.

My locker was located in the middle building, so I would have to return to that building between classes. Coming and going, these girls tripped me in the hallway, at least once a day.

As time went by, the attacks accelerated. The girls became more confrontational, especially one girl in particular. She seemed determined to end my life. This school was one bad place and the teachers had no control, whatsoever. Even the principal's new car got keyed, one morning.

As part of my lessons in Home Economics, I made a cute little sundress. When I brought it home, to show my mother, she made me rip out every seam. Then she taught me how to sew, properly.

Our final grade came on the day we modeled our dresses for our parents. It was after that class and just before school let out, that this jealousy from these other girls, came to a head. It had rained, earlier that day, and puddles of muddy water were everywhere.

Just as I approached the outer door to the building where my locker was, one of those girls tripped me. My knees hit the mud, ruining my dress. My books had also fallen into the muddy water. My parents would have to pay for those books.

With money so rare, in our family, this dress was precious to me. It was the prettiest thing I had ever owned.

Never before, had I experienced such a rage. I felt as though someone had put blinders on me. I suddenly had tunnel vision and 'seeing red' made sense.

I reached around and grabbed the girl by her hair, slung her around until she faced the pole that held up the awning. With my other hand, I grabbed the pole, and then began smashing her face into it.

Soon, we were both in the mud, beating each other in the face. A crowd gathered around us and soon there was also the principal, who stood there saying, "Now, girls".

In my rage, I sat up off the girl, with my fist still poised in the air and said back to him, "You want some of this?" at which, he backed off with a stupefied look on his face.

There never was a punishment for what had happened. This was already a lawless school.

The next day, as I stood in line for lunch, a cute little redhead came to stand with me. She said, "I hear you finished the war, yesterday".
"Huh?"
"You know, of course, you're the hero of the school, now."
"Huh?"

Just then, the very girl I had beat to a pulp, came up from behind me. She reached her arm around my waste, as though we were the best of buddies and say, "How ya doin today?"
"Huh?" I had no idea how to act.

I was learning a lot of hard lessons about some very strange characters. I was hardly a gang personality, and the last thing on my mind was this constant fighting. It just was not in my nature but these kids would not leave me alone.

Regardless of what it took, I was glad the war was over. I was tired of looking over my shoulder. Now, there was peace at last.

Chapter 7

My nagging about Winnie got on Willie's nerves. Finally, one day, she saddled up Winnie, just to shut me up. She thought that if I just saw the reality of this horse, I would abandon the idea. She rode Winnie and I rode Starlight. That seemed simple enough.

The ride was short. Winnie was excitable and just wanted to run. Willie was so worn out from Winnie's constant pull on the reigns; she got off and walked the last block to home. There was just no controlling that horse.

Winnie was all lathered up from a short walk around the block. She strained continuously, against the reigns. It was such a struggle just to hold this horse down to a gentle walk. The fact is, I never did witness a gentle walk, with this horse.

No one had ever succeeded in getting a bit in Winnie's mouth and resorted to using a hackamore. Usually a bit is used to apply pressure to the horses tongue, for control. A hackamore pinches from both sides of the nose, blocking off the wind. Sometimes, it's the only way to control a horse as stubborn as Winnie was.

Winnie was wild about running. That's all she wanted to do. No matter how hard and long the rider pulled back on those reigns, Winnie pushed to run. It was a non-stop battle just to hold her at a walk, which usually turned into a sideways canter.

This, of course, was no laughing matter. Winnie was one massive hunk of horseflesh. She stood 16 hands high and weighed over 1200 pounds. She was one big horse with muscles to go with it. She was, without a doubt, a beauty to behold. Winnie was tall enough, that to reach the stirrup, we had to find something to climb up onto. Don't you know, Winnie took advantage of that, more than once.

Sometimes, she would stand there patiently, just until a foot pushed weight onto the saddle. Before the rider could get a good seat, she was off and running, taking her one chance to take control.

Sometimes, out of pure orneriness, she would wait just until that first foot was in the stirrup, then side step, leaving the rider stretched out in mid-air, doing the splits.

It was never a point of her not being trained but more like a mischievous child pulling a prank.

Winnie was a sweet and loving horse but she had one problem. She just didn't understand a relaxing walk. To ride Winnie, was to fight her every step of the way or let her take her head and run. We joked that Winnie had two gears: Stop and Go.

I asked Willie, one day, "How can she keep going that way when she isn't getting any air?"
Willie shrugged her shoulders and said, "I have no idea. Sometimes I think she has a reserve tank, somewhere".

It took several days for Willie to finally relinquished and let me mount Winnie. What a ride. Now I understood what Willie had tried to tell me. I was worn out just from holding back, all the way.

While riding along the highway, if Winnie saw another horse even a mile ahead of us, she had to pass that horse. She was blind to anything but passing that other horse. Truly, she was insane. I couldn't help but imagine her on the track.

As time went by, Winnie became 'my' horse. There was a great friendship between us and we even spent time, out in the pasture, playing tag. Of course, when she tagged me, it was painful, as she would reach out and nip me in the rear. I learned that tight jeans were safer than loose pants.

It started when one day, I took both horses out to the pasture, to let them mow down the grass and spend time romping. As Winnie passed through the gate, I slapped her hard on the rump. She in turn, tossed her head, snorted, whipped around and came after me. I, of course, ran. She chased after me and nipped me on the seat of the pants, then suddenly jerked around and pretended to run from me. I chased after her and slapped her on the rump then ran off in the opposite direction. We had a new game. I remember a few times when I had to hide my jeans from my mother. She would have had a fit, to see the rip.

Winnie and I grew closer, and I began to understand how she thought and acted under different circumstances. It seemed to me, this was the most intelligent horse in the world. In fact, both horses had personality to spare.

Starlight scuffed his leg on something. We never did figure out how it happened. We dressed and bandaged his leg. Winnie spent the next few days, sniffing at his leg and then hanging her head over his neck. It was as though, she sympathized and was trying to comfort him.

Others told me things like, "Oh, Judy. You sure can read a lot into a horse!" To which I would reply, "It's not my imagination. I see it with my own eyes. You never pay attention, do you?"

Most of the summer was spent with Willie and me off on adventures by horseback: sometimes riding down to the river. Sometimes we went riding all around the area, collecting other girls and their horses, to join the crowd.

One particular day, we had ridden the 2 miles to our friend's house to invite her to come along. She had a gorgeous Buckskin stallion.

The last thing on our minds was that Winnie was in heat so we were in for quite an eventful afternoon. Imagine how embarrassed a bunch of teenaged girls were, when the stallion mounted Winnie with me on her. I screamed, "Hey! Get off me! Hey! Hey!" as a horse hoof knocked against the back of my head.

There's nothing like a bunch of silly girls. It took three

mountings, to convince us this was not the day for a ride with the neighbor. To make matters worse, these scenes all took place in full view of rush hour traffic, traveling down the highway.

One of the girls, at our school, had a Shetland pony that she insisted no one could ride. We got into an argument one day, about the possibility of a Shetland pony being such a twit. I said, "Are you kidding me? I mean, you're feet are still on the ground! What's so impossible about that?" Everybody was laughing and so you know, I had to take my turn at it.

The next day, after school, the bet was on. I only had $2 but I put it up for grabs, if I couldn't ride that tiny little pony. About five of us girls, all went straight to Shelly's back yard, where she kept this little pony. He sure looked docile enough.

With nothing more than a bridle, I straddled that pony. Both my feet were on the ground, I still had clearance between his back and me. I just stood there a second and then turned to say something to the girls, when all of a sudden I was face down on the ground, 3 feet in front of this little pony. "How did *that* happen?"

I got up, dusted myself off and turned around to stare at that 'short piece of nothing', grazing off a patch of grass. "What the...." Naturally, you know how it goes; I had to run that one through again, if for no other reason than to find out what had happened the first time.

I straddled that little stinker again. Both feet were still firmly on the ground. I slowly lowered my weight onto this pony's back. Just as I was seated, that little power-packed dynamo, raised up his rear so hard, it jet propelled me out and over his head again. A third try and I gave up the $2 and walked away, scratching my head.

Chapter 8

Life was not just horses for Willie and me. Every now and then, we hitched a ride on the city bus and rode downtown for a day of snooping and shopping. We never had much more than $5 but we managed to have a filled day of adventure, anyway. There was always the matinee at the movie theatre.

Back then, down town was still down town. Sears was still there and the dime store. There were café's and trinket shops. We had 3 city blocks, filled with shops and we ventured into every one of them.

I will never forget this strange habit of Willie's. Even while snooping through clothes racks, she would reach up to her scalp, scratch a little, then stick that fingernail in her mouth. What was she doing? I never asked but you know, I wondered about it. What ever, it didn't matter. I loved her anyway.

Daddy's garden was so productive; there was no possible way for us to eat everything that came off the vines and bushes. The back yard area was huge, about 100 feet long and 10 feet wider than the house, on each side.

My dad seemed to have magic fingers, when it came to plants. When we first moved in, he rented a garden tiller and tilled the entire back yard. He planted 6 rows of corn, with green beans planted between the stalks.

There was an abundance of radishes, tomatoes, and squash of all sorts, bell peppers and chili peppers, turnips, lettuce. He didn't forget a thing we loved to eat.

Our next-door neighbor, Mrs. Cota, was the elementary school cook. She did her own cooking every Friday. She readied a huge pot full of chili sauce, stacks of tortillas. She froze whole ingredients for quick meals, to last her the week.

With our huge abundance, we made a swap with her. We delivered baskets full of chili peppers and vegetables and she delivered pots full of chili. I'm not sure who got the best end of that deal. Her cooking was scrumptious.

Feeding our family dog was my chore. One day, I went out to the back porch with his bowl in hand but couldn't find the dog. I finally spied him, on Mrs. Cota's back porch. He was eating something out of a bowl.

I went to get him and thinking he was eating something she had set out to cool, I called her out to the porch. She informed me that the bowl was for Rusty and not to worry.

Then I noticed that it was hot chili, he was eating. My jaw dropped as I realized the reason he was whimpering, while he ate, was because of hot chilies. "Oh, my god!"
"Oh, not to worry. He's fine. He does that every Friday."
"What? How long has he been over here bugging you?"
"He's no bother, to me. He loves my chili. He's been coming over here for his snack, for the past 3 weeks."
"What?" I stared down at Rusty, in disbelief. Then it dawned on me that I hadn't seen Rusty throw up, in over a week. Little Rusty had a physical problem he couldn't help.

We obtained the dog when he was only 4 weeks old. Some neighbor's dog had puppies and we children fell in love. The neighbor's promised us, one of the puppies, as soon as they were weaned.

The problem was, it was hot summer and these people kept the puppies outside, in a box. Maggots got to the puppies. The children visited, every day, so when maggots began to show sores all over the puppies, we ran to tell mother.

Mother was a nurse and could handle some pretty awful sights. When she saw the condition of the puppies, she told the owner that we would take our puppy now, before they all died. Then mother took the puppy to the vet, who gave her some ointment to use.

This ointment, blocked off the air to the maggots, causing them to rise to the surface. The only way to get rid of them was to pick them off as they popped up. This, mother had to do every hour until they were all gone.

This poor tiny puppy went through pure hell. Every hour, mother applied the ointment then sat waiting, with tissue in hand. I had to help hold the puppy still, while she squeezed to get just 'one more'.

Day after day, this went on, until finally the last maggot was gone. That poor little puppy suffered so much, and so early in life.

The maggots had gotten into 2 places on one ear, 1 place on the other ear and in her navel. Because of that life start, Rusty had a life long problem. When he got excited, he threw up.

For the most part, he was an outside dog because every time we let him come in the house, he got so excited, he heaved. It was just something we lived with, knowing how it all started.

Now, of all the things, this dog was eating chili. This kind of rocked my boat because it did not make sense. We had to be so careful with what he ate because his poor little body could not tolerate certain things. Now, without our knowledge, the neighbor had been feeding him things we never would have dreamt.

I thought back over the past few days and realized I hadn't seen him throw up, in all that time. I went home with the tale.

Just to test him, we let him in the house. We were amazed when he didn't throw up, just because he got excited. What was this? Did chilies heal him?

Chapter 9

Marvelous and strange things happened during that year. Even my little sister, got into the act.

She had decided that instead of eating her Easter eggs, she would save them, because they were so pretty. They were hardly pretty a month later. I reached up on the top shelf of our closet, to get something and this little box fell out. When it did, one of two eggs blew up, all over the closet. There's nothing like the aroma of a rotten egg.

After the initial shock, I very carefully picked up the other egg. I gently cradled it in my open palms, while I slowly walked out to the burn barrel. Just as I was turning my hand to let the egg drop into the barrel, it blew up in my face. Oh, what a smell! Little sisters are such a delight.

Linda was a girl that lived on a small alfalfa farm, just beyond the irrigation ditch, behind my house. She was another one of the girls, making up a lasting memory in this chapter of my life. I will never forget this character, mostly because of her home.

I had never seen a home so cluttered, so piled up or with so much *stuff* in my life. I could have sworn that the boots, her dad wore out 20 years ago, were still there in the pile. How did these people live? Where was the dinner table? I didn't know a couch could be so swayback that a body could disappear, just by sitting down. Saddles sat in the corner of the kitchen. Under the pile on the kitchen table, was another pile of saddle blankets. Nothing made sense, in this house.

Linda, for sure, was one unique girl. She wore cowboy boots and jeans, to school. Her long hair was tightly braided into pigtails. Both she and her horse were short runts. That was a match.

I don't know what breed this horse was. He was not as small as a Welch and certainly not the size of a Quarter horse. He was something in between. Maybe that was the point.

His mane was roached (cut short) and pretty much matched his personality. Everywhere we rode together, we had to look down to talk to Linda.

One day, Willie and I rode over to Linda's house to gather her up for a long ride. Linda asked if I wanted to ride her horse, just to see how he felt. I mounted that little horse and just as I was getting settled, Linda took the ends of the reigns and slapped the horse ears. All of a sudden, I was in a rodeo, as this little horse first raised his rump, then dove his head toward the ground, and then switched ends. His rump went down and his head came up so hard, he smacked me in the mouth, hard enough to draw blood. Before I could catch my breath, he went through the same routine. It's called 'fish tailing' and this little horse was beating me up. His rump would hit the back of my head and then his head would pound my face.

To end the ride of my life, I simply gave up and slid off the side. Boy was I mad. Linda was laughing so hard, over her little joke, tears were pouring down her face. She thought that was funny! Then I learned that was a quirk with this little horse. He couldn't stand to have his ears slapped. She had done that on purpose.

Needless to say, there was no riding that day. I had to go home and clean up, as there was blood, sweat and tears all over my face, hair and clothes.

As crazy as it sounds, the next morning, I mounted and rode that horse. It turned out, he was a great little jumper but I never rode him out on the street. I didn't have *much* sense but I did have *that* much.

The summer wore on and we girls whiled away our time on horse back. Several times, we packed up the saddle bags with a can of Pork n Beans, a loaf of bread and water, and rode off for a day along the river.

Winnie was a strange bit of horseflesh. She would shy away from a tiny trickle of water but when it came to that river, she plunged in with pure delight. This is where I got into trouble, every time we ventured across that river. Winnie wanted to lie down in the water, with me on her, not to mention a loaf of bread. What a fight, to keep her on her feet. In desperation, I would slap her ears with the reigns and threaten her life, if she lay down. "Huh-uh…no, Winnie. No, Winnie."

I lost that fight, a few times. Down we went. Winnie was in heaven but I was soaked to the bone and I sure didn't appreciate what she was doing to my boots. The river was only about 2 feet deep, where we crossed. There was plenty of room to keep my feet high and dry. My vocabulary grew that summer. "Dammit, horse! Dammit, dammit, dammit, stop! Oh, you damn horse!"

Winnie was such a challenge to ride; one would have to ponder why this young girl was so determined to get along with her. At the very least, an hour's ride took all my energy just to keep things under control.

It seemed to me, we two girls were always getting into some kind of trouble. We ventured out to ride across the plain, one day. We needed to cross the freeway, as we went. We decided that we could make it through one of those concrete tunnels that run under the highway. It was certainly high enough for the horses to pass through but not high enough with us on the horses. We got down and walked through the little tunnel.

Half the way through, Starlight began to get agitated. He was frightened by the closed in feeling. He pulled back on his haunches and we tugged to get him to finish walking through. Then he did the unthinkable. He reared up, knocking his head against the top of the tunnel, then down he went. He was knocked cold. "Oh, rats!" While he was still half stupefied by the blow, we managed to get him up on his feet. We scooted back out of that tunnel, as fast as we could make him move and decided never to try that one again.

Then there was the day Willie and I, riding double and bareback, took Starlight out for a stroll across some ranch land. When we came upon a cow, we decided to see what it was like to ride one. Since I was riding behind Willie, I tried it first. We trotted up along side of this cow and I jumped off the horse, landing on what felt something like the edge of a 2X4 board. Ouch!

The cow started to move and then panicked and began to run. I began screaming at Willie, "Get me off this thing!" After several attempts to come along side and help me change mounts, I just gave up and fell off. I had discovered something worse than Starlight's spine.

Willie decided she just *had* to try this, for herself. She got behind me, on Starlight. We again, rode up along side that poor cow and she jumped off, landing on the cow's back. "Ah, ha! See there? I told you!" as Willie slid off the right side of the cow, groaning in pain.

As she pulled herself up and dusted herself off, she said, "Ugh! Gees! You're right! Oh man, I've never felt anything quite like *that*!" Ok, so we didn't bother any more cows. Once was enough.

There was a huge field full of tall sunflowers that we passed each day, coming home from school. On one of our ventures, we road down that little side street, where the sunflowers grew.

A sudden, sideways jolt and Winnie was plunging into the sunflowers and ran the full length of the field, coming out on the other side. I happened to be wearing shorts and a sleeveless blouse. The plants stood as tall as my shoulders and prickly little spurs on the stems, clawed my skin nearly off. My skin was red and burning like fire.

You probably already know that as we disappeared into the sunflowers, my screams and curses could be heard a block away. I still don't know why she did that. It must have been something I did. She was always giving me 'what for'.

Chapter 10

Willie asked me one day, "Would you mind taking care of the horses while we go on vacation?"

"Of course! When you going?"

"We'll be gone, over the Christmas holidays. About 2 weeks."

"Sure thing. Don't worry about it. I'll take care of everything."

As far as I was concerned, she knew better than to ask. We were like sisters and all she was asking was for me to continue with our every day routine.

Winnie and Starlight were used to the routine of daily rides and adventures. I let them take turns, one day I took Winnie and the next day I took Starlight. Each day, I groomed and petted, then saddled and went off for a day of riding. The horses loved the attention and we grew closer.

It was as though Winnie knew all witnesses were gone. Her very first turn to be alone with me for the day, she started her shenanigans.

I rode down the street to the highway, crossed over the pavement, headed for that wide dirt shoulder. Just as we stepped off the pavement, Winnie jolted into a dead run, ran straight toward the clear ditch. Just at the edge of the ditch, she stopped short, ducked her head down and pitched me straight off her back, landing me dead center of the ditch.

At this time of the year, tumbleweeds filled the ditch,

clear to the top. At the bottom, was muddy ice. I plunged down the center, all the way down through those tumble weeds, landing with my bottom in nasty, black sludgy ice. I looked up through the hole in the weeds that I had just created, dreading the trip up the side of the ditch.

Not knowing what Winnie was up to, and the knowledge that we were right next to a busy highway, drove me to climb out, as fast as I could get it done. I put my head down to protect my face, against those prickly tumbleweeds, and started climbing. As I reached the top, pushing tumbleweeds up at the surface, I raised my face to view Winnie's nose. She stood there waiting and watching.

Oh, that damn horse! *What?* Was she getting a kick out of this? I pushed myself up and out of the ditch, just as Winnie jerked her head up. She tossed herself about and began trotting away, headed straight for the highway. I ran after her, to catch her before she reached the pavement but she just kept playing the 'keep away' game, staying just ahead of me. When I sped up, she sped up. When I slowed down, she slowed down.

She crossed the highway, slowing traffic, with me right behind her. Half way down the side street, I finally caught hold of the reigns. Boy did it all come to a head, then. Nose to nose, eyeball to eyeball, the lecture started. She was no dummy. She knew what she did.

I was a miserable mess. There were dried tumbleweeds down my shirt, down my panties! Icy mud was all up my back. I have no idea what my hair looked like and at that moment, I didn't care. That was the end of this day's ride. I went home, cleaned up, then went back to collect Starlight.

With Winnie neighing and snorting at me, in disbelief, I saddled up Starlight and we went off for a leisure ride.

The next day was still Starlight's turn. Just because Winnie caused such a storm, the day before, ending her day out, didn't mean today wasn't still his turn. I brought Starlight out of the pen and began to groom him. All the while, Winnie stretched her neck over the top of the fence, letting me know she didn't think this was fair. She wanted out. She wanted to go somewhere. I ignored her and pampered Starlight, in defiance.

Starlight and I went on a wonderful, soft, pleasant ride and stretched out the time, as much as possible. Of course, that was a problem for me. While it was pleasurable, it was also boring but I wasn't going to cut it short. Winnie had to learn.

The next day, I ventured over to the paddock, not knowing what I would face this time. Who knew what that crazy horse would do to me.

As I came through the fence and headed for the gate to the pen, Winnie pushed up against the gate, blocking Starlight's way. She was positively letting me know, this was *her* day, not Starlight's. "Ok, ok", I cooed at her. "I'm not forgetting and I'm not punishing you any more. You're going for a ride, today, so calm down."

I brought her out to the tack room then decided this was the day she was going to wear a bridle. At first, I tried to just trick her into it but that didn't work. Those teeth clamped down and she backed away, defiantly. I even tried to force the bit into her mouth but she was too strong for me.

I finally got tired of the game, slipped off the halter and put the hackamore on her nose, just as she lifted her left front foot, and slyly placed it on my toe. Then she leaned into me hard, throwing me off balance. I was trapped. She had me off balance enough; I had no strength to push back. All I could do was pound on her shoulder and scream, "Winnie! Winnie-e-e-e-e! Get off!" I don't really know how much time passed, with this horse leaning all her weight against me, with my foot trapped under her hoof.

When she finally leaned away from me, letting me pull loose, I was furious with her. "Oh, no! No more of this! You're staying!" Back went the halter and I led her straight back to the paddock. I pushed her inside then grabbed Starlight.

Again, Starlight and I went for a ride, instead of Winnie. There was no way, I was going to reward her for her actions. She could just stew in her own misery, as far as I was concerned. "Shame on you, Winnie!"

By the time we got back from our ride, Winnie was a nervous wreck. She charged the gate, while I was trying to put Starlight back in. She tossed her head, at me and snorted, then charged around the pen, letting me know how unhappy she was. I didn't care and I let her know. I turned my back on her, while I put the saddle away and cleaned up.

The next day, things got really interesting. It was like two women at battle. I stood outside the pen and just stared at Winnie. "What's it going to be, today? Huh? We going to be friends or are we going to fight?" Winnie stood along the fence, opposite me and ignored me. Nothing. No storming around. No snorting. No pushing at the gate. Just nothing.

Starlight, on the other hand, was excited and wanted to go for a ride but I decided Winnie had been punished enough. I went in and led her out. It was almost spooky, as she walked out as docile as a lamb. Something was up but I didn't know what, so I went about my business of brushing her back.

I combed her hair, pretty, gave her a bite of oats and gave her a little kiss on the nose. I hoped the battle was over and we could be friends, today.

Nothing. No signs. No bad girl. Anybody else, in that situation, would have enough sense to back off and rethink but not me. Oh, no not me. Just kept pushing forward and acting as if everything was back to normal.

I saddled her, mounted up and rode out. We rode down the little neighborhood street and out to the highway. We crossed the highway and were gingerly walking along when all of a sudden the world exploded.

Winnie began bucking and when she bucked, it was

serious. If there was anything about that horse that told you she came from racing blood, it was that super long back of hers. Her back was so long that the gentlest gait was the trot. When she was at a dead run, you'd think your back would never be straight again. It was impossible to get into her rhythm. Her trot was so long gaited; it was like riding a rocking chair.

Bucking was another matter. She could deliver quite a wallop with that long swing, at your backside. She dove her head down and that rump came up so hard, I flew. She waited until we were half the way across the highway, to deliver the final blow. I landed right under her belly.

She froze and waited, right there in the second lane during rush hour traffic. She couldn't do this away from public view. Oh, no! She pulled this off in a crowd of cars, with a whole lot of curious witnesses.

My glasses flew off my face and now I was half-blind and squinting, as I searched around the ground. I didn't move, the horse didn't move. I finally spied my glasses about 6 feet off to the left of Winnie's head. I dove, as fast as I could, toward the glasses. As soon as I was visible to her, she bolted off. I grabbed my glasses, put them back on and the chase was on, again. "Dammit, horse! Just dammit!" It was a miracle we hadn't both been hit by a speeding car. Just unbelievable!

Of course, the ride was cut short again and Starlight reaped the benefits. When was Winnie going to catch on, that when she pulled off her little tricks, she lost out?

Chapter 11

The next day, I was determined that Winnie and I were going for a ride. This time, I was going to win. She wasn't going to get away with her tantrums, any more.

Getting to know Winnie was a love-hate situation. I couldn't help admiring her spirit. This was a horse that lived to run. Without running, life had no meaning for her and yet there was no proper place to let her take her head and run to her hearts content. She was untrained and unruly.

At the age of 4, she needed special attention but who would ever take on the job. Her owners didn't seem to care. There was no real purpose in training her, as she would never be raced. It was a sad situation and I had no control, what so ever.

I was barely more than a child, had no money of my own and nobody to side with me. The only thing I had was love for this dear horse.

We rode north, up the highway, about 5 miles from the house. So far, so good. As I was turning her around, ready to come back, a truck driver speeding down the highway spotted me and blew his air horn.

Winnie bolted into a dead run, so fast that I lost my grip on the reigns. With reigns flying, I held on to the saddle horn for dear life, while I reached out trying to grasp the reigns as they flew by.

It's hard to explain, exactly what that felt like. Her back was the longest I had ever personally witnessed. Each stride brought a hard jolt throughout my body.

With the proper saddle and setup, the rider is standing in the stirrups, with his weight shifted up to the horse's shoulders. This was no racing saddle. It was a western saddle and the stirrups adjusted to give the rider about a 2-inch gap, to the seat. Those 2 inches was not enough protection from what this horse could do to me. There was no possible way to shift away from the hard slap to the spine.

Reaching forward, trying to get hold of the reigns, while all this was going on, was an impossible nightmare and this horse was running away. As far as I could determine, she was panicked.

I had personally witnessed this horse clocked at over 38 miles per hour and she was working harder now, than ever before. This was a dangerous combination. I was afraid for Winnie, as much as for myself. There was no slowing her down. She wasn't tiring.

About a mile down the road, there was a crossing neighborhood street, a bridge and stop sign. Just as we neared that crossing road, a man driving a yellow Volkswagen, drove up and stopped at the sign. He looked to his right, checking traffic, but just as he turned his head to look off to the left, his eyes bugged out at the sight of horse and rider, no more than 30 feet away and headed straight for him, at a dead run.

I saw my life flash before my eyes, because I had never seen Winnie jump. I just *knew* she was going to pull her little trick of dashing off to one side, leaving me to fly forward over that Volkswagen. I started screaming, "Winnie, stop! Stop it! You're going to kill us! Stop! You can't jump! No! No!" to no avail because, at that moment I was just along for the ride.

I never felt her feet leave the ground. Everything happened so fast. My mind couldn't keep up with what was happening. I looked down, just in time to see wide-open, unbelieving eyes and a gaping mouth, as we flew over the top of that little car.

Now I was in an even bigger panic, not knowing if she could land safely. Every quarter second, I envisioned myself lying out on the ground, mangled. Who knew what condition Winnie would be in. My heart raced, knowing that still....the reigns were a threat as they flew along in the wind. What will happen if she somehow stepped on the reigns as she landed? What if, her legs are not strong enough? What if......

I wish I could describe what the landing felt like. I don't know. I never felt an impact. All I knew was that I looked down, saw this black face turn white, I saw the yellow top of the Volkswagen, I braced for a fall but it didn't happen. Before I could record that sight in my mind, we were another half mile down the road and still at a dead run.

Now we were headed toward a busy intersection, with a traffic light. I had to get her under control. I finally grabbed hold of the left reign and started pulling down hard on her head. With her head pulled down to her chest, she kept running. I was beginning to panic. I had to get her to stop. Somehow, someway, she had to be stopped.

In desperation, and knowing I was liable kill myself, I lifted my right leg, as though to dismount. That did the trick. I finally learned what it took to stop Winnie. I dismounted in mid stride. I learned to hang on for dear life, while raising my leg and then bringing it back down toward the ground, as though to dismount. That, for some odd reason, caused Winnie to come to a sudden stop.

I climbed down and walked around to look Winnie in the eye. Her heart was pounding, she was lathered up and her eyes still held panic. It wasn't a dirty trick, after all. She had truly spooked and jolted. I certainly learned to hate those truck drivers and their loud horns. "Oh, my poor Winnie." I talked to her in a soothing voice and rubbed her nose until she calmed down enough to move on. I didn't climb back into the saddle. Winnie needed a friend not a rider. We walked together while I talked calmly to her, all the way home.

We were almost home when it suddenly hit me, what she had done. I turned around, looked her straight on, and said, "Winnie! You jumped!" Oh, man, had she jumped.

Chapter 12

When I returned Winnie to the pen, Starlight got it in his head that it was his turn to go bye-bye and tried to come out the gate as I was pushing Winnie in. After all, that was the usual routine. I would leave with Winnie then come back to get him, after she had tried to kill me. This was the end of the day and I convinced Starlight to go back in. Tomorrow was another day.

The next morning, the strangest thing happened. Just as I passed through the gate, Starlight was standing against the opposite side. He turned and looked at me. If looks could kill, I was already dead. His ears went straight back and he raised his upper lip, showing me his teeth. He then lowered his head and dove straight toward me, leading with those teeth. He was charging me! "Uh, uh....Starlight?" I ran for the gate but he was too fast. I could feel his breath on my backside, as I literally flew over the top of the gate.

Sitting outside, on the ground, I peered through the boards at Starlight. My first thought was to look for foam around the mouth. This was the docile horse! This was the kind gentleman! What was going on?

"Starlight? What's the matter, boy?" He reared up and twisted around, trotting off to the other side of the pen. I rose up and dusted myself off then just stood there. I didn't know what to do, with this situation. I'd never seen Starlight act this way. He was mad at me but for what!

All this, was going way too far. Two jealous horses? I thought, "Oh, this is just too crazy". When I tried to enter the pen again, Starlight dove at me with those teeth, a second time. This time, I ran around the post that held up a lean to, and caught him around the neck.

As he was pulling back, trying to get rid of me, I was hollering at him, "Hold it, boy. Hey! Hold it! What's the matter with you?" After a few seconds, he calmed down and lowered his head. I went eyeball to eyeball, asking him, "Baby, what's the matter?"

The only thing that could possibly make sense is that he had thought, the night before, that he was going to get his turn and it didn't happen. I truly think he was mad at me.

I brought him out to the tack room and began brushing him down. Every few seconds, he stretched his neck around to watch me, while I groomed him. "Aw, poor baby. Winnie's got us all crazy. I'm sorry. Wanna go bye-bye, now?"

Was it my imagination or was this animal jealous? Starlight was a whole new horse, that day. During the entire time we rode out together, he held his head high and he strutted. You'll never convince me that horse wasn't trying to impress me that day.

The next day, I went back to that very spot where Winnie had flown over the top of that Volkswagen. The little side street was only about 20 feet wide but it blew my mind, realizing Winnie had never so much as touched the pavement. Peering down at the ground, where she had landed, I noted where her hind feet had dug into the ground harder than her front feet. She had barely touched the ground with her front feet. She was still digging in, still running with all her might. All of my intelligence mustered up a , "Wow" as I pondered what had happened.

The gang type girls at school took advantage of Willie's absence. She wasn't back from vacation yet and school had started up again, after the Christmas holidays. As I was walking along a small ditch, behind the houses, on my way home, one of those girls suddenly appeared and threatened me, saying, "You better watch it, bitch! I won't be alone, next time". Then she just walked away.

The next day, just after school let out, I was walking along the outer fence of the schoolyard. There was no sidewalk on this side of the street, just a wide dirt area between the little road and the school fence. I looked up to see about 20 boys, with that same girl, all lined up across the dirt area to block my path. Evidently, she had gathered reinforcements to attack me.

I thought about crossing the road but I knew they would just cross over, with me. I held my ground. I had no choice. Knowing these kids, the way I did, I knew better than to try running. If I turned around and went the other way, the race would be on and I would lose.

I was the unusual twirp, in their world. While the little Mexican girls had long black hair, mine was red and very short, cut into a ducktail. I didn't carve some boy's initials into my arms. I didn't load myself down with jewelry. I didn't wear makeup. I was totally the opposite of these girls.

My arms were loaded down with a stack of books, my one and only defense. I raised the books high up to my chest, raised my nose in the air and marched right through the crowd of boys, while the girl screamed profanities at them for not killing me.

The boys didn't know what to do with this gutsy girl, who barely acknowledged their existence. They just parted the waters, so to speak, and let me pass.

This is the day I learned a huge lesson. For a confrontation to come to fruition, one had to either show fear or act as though ready for a fight. Otherwise, they didn't know what to do or when.

It was about that time, I discovered a switchblade in my father's desk. It was a souvenir from his days in the military, when he went over seas. I took it without asking, and carried it for self-defense, from that day on.

Chapter 13

The next time I took Winnie out for a ride, I decided to find out just what it would take to tire this horse. I rode out onto the mesa, where there was nothing but sand and sagebrush. Not exactly a kind riding path but it certainly would be a good place to help Winnie blow off some steam.

A 'mesa' (a Spanish term) is the common language of the area, describing a flat plain area. With miles of open range in front of us, I tied the ends of the reigns together. Then I lifted up the knotted end, where Winnie could see and said, "See this?" then dropped the reigns over the saddle horn.

I didn't have to prompt her. She was off to the imagined races. I was in for one rough ride. Even at a dead run, she dodged back and forth around the bigger bushes and jumped the smaller ones. It seemed more like a game for her. I just hung on, waiting for her to be winded and come to a stop. It didn't happen.

I kept thinking, "She's bound to get tired and slow down". After several minutes of having my brains pounded, I suddenly got a strange feeling and grabbed the reigns. I began pulling down. Just pulling back, never accomplished a darn thing, with that horse. I had to pull her head down, hoping to make it too hard for her to see where she was going. It wasn't working.

You would think that using a hackamore and literally blocking off her wind would get her attention. It wasn't going to happen with this horse. She could keep running even without the wind. It was the rider, who eventually gave up on that idea, fearing what it would do to her.

Call it instinct, I don't know, but something told me there was danger ahead. I didn't see anything but I sure felt it. In desperation, I lifted my leg and Winnie came to a stop. About 8 feet ahead, there was a 4 foot drop off into an arroyo. "Well, rats!" Where on earth, could I go and let this horse loose to run until she was tired? "Winnie, baby, I'm trying."

I knew, instinctively, this horse should have been trained. She should have been living out her own dreams of running and running. That's all she was born to do.

Through the quarter-horse appearance, and the colors of a paint, I could see her grandfather. She was racing blood, through and through. Here she was, some girl's pet and worse, a neglected pet. I spent hours just sitting on a fence, admiring this thing of beauty that no one seemed to care about. What a waste. What a waste.

The world would never know of this seed of Man O War. They would never have the chance to see this horse run. That alone, was the pleasure of a lifetime.

I also spent time, letting the two horses out into the small pasture, just to watch them romp and play.

Seeing them together was better than television, any day.

Starlight seemed to be protective of his little 'sis' who was twice his size. He too, would kick up his heels just to spur her into a frenzy of bucking and running. If only I had had the foreknowledge to get a picture of her, while I still could. There is only one picture of me sitting on Starlight. That's it.

While I sat on the fence, watching, it was as if Winnie were a child, showing off for me. She would run and then suddenly stop, twist around and buck. She tossed her head and pranced around. I would clap my hands, in approval, which just sent her off again.

I swear she was the smartest horse that ever lived. That coming from a 14-year-old's point of view. I could say, "You wanna go for a ride?" and she was right there waiting for me to open the gate. If she was ready for a ride and I said, "Not today" she pulled her head up, in seemingly disbelief, and began backing up, to show her disapproval.

Chapter 14

Willie returned from vacation and life began to settle back into a routine. One thing was for sure, we would always take both horses, when we went riding. I told Willie about the things that happened while she was gone. Some of it, she believed, some she did not.

Nancy's birthday rolled around and all of us girls were invited to her party. We had a great time, cutting up, eating chips and coke and playing our 45 records. I heard "The Little Nash Rambler" for the first time.

That night provided lasting memories. Nancy's mom couldn't hold out and fell asleep, long before we girls were ready to call it a night. Then Nancy got a wild idea and we all piled into her mother's car.

None of us knew how to drive and argued, for the longest time, who would be the victim to climb behind the wheel. They all looked at me.

"Oh no, not me! I can't drive!" I whined back at them.
"Aw, come on….Somebody has to do it!" All the girls were chirping at each other, giggling and prodding. At last, I gave in, climbed behind the wheel and turned the key. What a rush!

I was scared, half out of my wits but determined this couldn't possibly be as hard as all that. I somehow managed to get the car backed out of the driveway, grateful that we were at the end of the street, where no other cars might come by. The whole neighborhood was long gone to sleep.

We crept along, about 10 miles per hour, down the long, dark street until we reached the last possible turn before the highway. I almost didn't get slowed down enough to make the turn and all the girls were screaming and yelling out instructions. "More, more. Turn it some more!"

"No, no! Back....turn back....screech!....you're gonna hit that fence!"

"Ok, back to the right....No! left, left!"

"Stop! Stop! Put your foot on the brake. No! The brake!!"

"Ok, now let's go but be more careful, this time. We're doing just fine, you'll see."

"Ok, now left at this next street. Left! Left! Dammit!" Slaps across the neck, while girls panicked in the back seat.

Nancy, breathless from screaming said, "I think we better try to get back to the house. This is scarier than I thought it would be."

So we made it down the length of that neighboring street, made another left and crept back into the driveway.

We all climbed out, grateful to still be alive. Now there was a screaming hissy, as we all blamed each other. There's nothing quite like a bunch of 13 and 14 year old girls, shaking off a huge dose of dread and excitement. The party was over.

It seemed, at the time, that this routine would go on forever. Sadly, it was about to come to an end. Not our friendship. Willie and I would go on being friends for years. The routine, with both Starlight and Winnie, though, was about to change.

Willie's parents decided to sell Winnie. Their eldest daughter was no longer interested and they saw no good reason to keep her. My heart was breaking.

I surely didn't have the money to buy her and my parents gave me a stern, "No". It wasn't as easy as all that. Every day, I brought up the subject. I'm sure; I was the family nagger for quite some time.

"Daddy, pleeeaase! There's just *got* to be a way. You don't understand! There's just *got* to be a way." I spent hours, sitting out in the vegetable garden, crying. I couldn't understand how the world could be so cruel.

My dad's reply was, "We don't have a place to keep a horse. Where are you going to keep her, in the garden? Think about it, Judy. Even the septic tank is only covered by boards. You can't put a horse where they could fall into the septic tank! Right?"

"But daddy. The Morrison's love me and they wouldn't care....I could keep her right there, where she is now. As long as I was feeding her and taking care of her, and they didn't have to bother. They would let me do that." But still, the answer was "no".

I was afraid of what would happen to Winnie. Would she be loved and appreciated? All my pleading, fell on deaf ears.

I felt so helpless and small. Anxiety was my closest companion until the day came that I heard it was Mary's dad, who wanted to buy her. I thought, "At the very least, we can visit her". I wanted to watch over her and make sure she had a good life. No one understood Winnie, the way I did and I knew there was liable to be trouble ahead.

A few days passed. Willie and I busied ourselves, keeping Starlight occupied. He was lonely without his companion and he was already becoming an 'old man' because of his loss. Maybe we were silly girls, but we could swear we saw depression all over him.

It had been only a couple days, when we took Starlight and rode over to the neighbor's house to visit Winnie. I saw her, at a distance, before we came close enough for her to see us. Her head was down. I had never seen her do that.

We called out to her, "Winnie! Hey, girl!" Her head tossed up in the air and she jerked around to see us coming.

She snorted and ran to the fence, where she and Starlight sniffed each other and both whinnied a greeting. We stepped down, petted her nose, and asked how she was doing.

Another week passed and we again went to visit. This time, our hearts sank as we laid eyes on marks across her nose. While we were there, stroking Winnie's nose, Mary came out her back door to say hello. We asked her what had happened to Winnie's nose. Mary told us, her father was trying to train her to polo.

"Polo? Winnie is a race horse. She'll never train to Polo! Well....what happened? Did she run into something?"

Mary lowered her head in shame and said, "He whipped her".
"With what! A wire!" by now, I was almost hysterical.
"With a clothes hanger." There was dead silence and then she added, "I'm sorry, girls. He got really, really mad at her."

After each visit, we went straight to Willie's parents to report what we saw. They seemed sad about it but did nothing. Our hands were tied.

Each time we went to visit, Winnie was in worse shape than the last visit. First, there were those marks across her nose. Then we witnessed scars across her back. I thought I'd die, when we saw marks across her belly. What was this man doing to our precious Winnie?

We went around to the front of the house, to visit with Mary. We gathered in her bedroom to whisper, outside of her parent's hearing.

Mary said, "There's a pond, where they play polo. It seems that when the game went right through the pond, Winnie laid down with my father still on her. He got so mad! I think he kicked her in the face, I'm not sure. When he got home, he took her out back, took away all her food and then he beat her with a board."

I said, through my tears, "Oh my god! What can we do? How can we stop this? It isn't fair!"

Willie and I went to her parents and begged them to help. All we got out of them was, "What can we do? We sold her to him. It's out of our hands."

Every visit, found Winnie's spirits lower than before and then we saw that she was loosing weight.

She was no longer the spirited race horse. She was beginning to look like an old nag and she was only 4 years old. What could we do?

This was long before the animal rights people, came along. Long before anyone would do anything about it. We were alone in our grief.

Chapter 15

My parents decided to move back up to the heights. I didn't know why. I never knew why. I just knew I was being ripped from the most wonderful time of my life and I didn't want to go.

Now back to the city streets, I felt nothing but sadness. I couldn't concentrate on my school studies. My only interests revolved around yesterday. Thank goodness for the distraction of 3 neighboring new friends.

My mother began having troubles of her own, which distracted me from my worries over Winnie. She kept getting these disabling migraine headaches, which lasted sometimes for 3 days.

Coming home from school, every day, turned into a 'hush-hush' affair, as I tiptoed into the door to make sure mother was up and about. When I found that her bedroom door was closed, I knew it was because she was blocking out light. I would quietly sneak into her room, to ask if she needed iced-tea. Most times, she depended on me and waited for me when I came home from school.

The migraines eventually turned worse and I was left to help mother, sometimes waiting on her hand and foot for days. During those times, I was the mother for the other two. It was hard to think about Winnie, and mourn days past.

Willie and I stayed in touch by phone. Between bouts with my mother, I managed to get down to the valley to see her, now and then. Only at those times, did I get an update on Winnie's situation.

Sometimes I would come spend the weekend with her. Once, she came to spend the night with me but something in the neighborhood irritated her allergies. We woke up the next morning to a fit of sneezing. When the constant sneezing didn't stop, even after lunch, we gave up and took her home.

During one of my weekend visits at Willie's house, we did something we would never forget. Her mother smoked these strange cigarettes called 'English Ovals'. She kept the carton in the freezer, as she didn't smoke enough to use them up before they dried out. The freezer kept them fresh.

We stole a pack of her mother's cigarettes and took them with us on a ride. It made us feel all grown up, to smoke a cigarette. Near the end of the day, we realized that we couldn't just take back a portion of a pack or her mother would catch on, to what we had done. We didn't want to waste them, so we worked hard at smoking every last one.

We managed to smoke them all but then for the whole next week, we both suffered with a horrible cough. On Wednesday, I called Willie and found out that she too, was having a horrid time with coughing. We both vowed never to do that again.

This was such a heart breaking time for me. I could no longer ride with Willie every day; no longer see Winnie. Winnie was in a miserable place and I couldn't do anything about it. I just kept calling Willie, and getting reports.

Finally, one day, I called and Willie reported that her parents had gone to witness for themselves. When they saw Winnie's condition, they offered to buy her back but the man refused. Even though, he had no use for her, he bull-headedly ignored their pleas and refused to let them take her. When they threatened to sue him, he gave in. They brought her home and began nursing her back to health.

I begged a ride to the valley, to see for myself. I walked out to the pen and just stood there for a few seconds. This was not Winnie. Was this Winnie? It couldn't be.

I ran back to the house and asked Willie's mom, "Are you sure that's Winnie?"
"Yes, dear. I'm afraid so. She's lost more than half her weight and I don't know if she will pull through."
Willie said, "Judy, she'll never be ridden again. That guy broke her leg and it didn't set the way it should. He just didn't care."

Oh, this just couldn't be happening. This powerful stead, reduced to a feeble old nag. I went back out to Winnie and reached out for her nose. "Winnie? Don't you recognize me? It's me! Oh, poor Winnie. What did he do to you?"

Her back was swayed. Her ribs were sticking out. Her bottom lip hung as though she couldn't control it any more. The fire was gone from her eyes and her coat was dull and patchy. She didn't move, just stood there hanging her head over the feed trough. I tried to hand feed her but it seemed she didn't have the energy even to reach out.

I couldn't stand it any more. I had to leave. A cloud hung over me, for weeks. I couldn't stop crying over the pitiful waste.

I called at least once a week, to check on Winnie's condition. She was gaining weight. The day came when Willie told me, "Winnie is beginning to recognize me, again". Oh what joyful news that was.

Chapter 16

It took a year, but the day finally came, the family took her out to a friend's ranch and let her go to pasture. About a year later, they felt she was strong enough and began breeding her. The last I heard, she had given birth to four potential racehorses. Then she was retired, to spend the rest of her days out to pasture.

It was almost 2 years later, I begged Willie's family to take me out to see her. When we drove up to a fence beside the road and stopped, I got out and peered across the field. I didn't see her, anywhere. "Are you sure, this is the right pasture?"

We got back into the car, and drove around the side of this huge pasture, then stopped again. I climbed out and searched all around but still couldn't see Winnie. I started getting scared. It had been a year, since the family last saw her. Maybe she was dead.

I screamed as loud as I could "Winnie! Hey! Winnie!" A head popped up, way on the other side of the pasture. She had been standing just down a hill, where I couldn't see.

"Oh, yes! Winnie. Winnie! Come'ere girl! Come here!" I clapped my hands, the way I used to, when she was showing off.

I heard her whinny and then start to run. As she came up the hill, into my sight, I thought my heart would burst. I was so happy to see. Winnie looked like her old self. She had gained the weight back and looked so strong, again. Then I saw a bonus. The young colt, running along behind. He was running and kicking, the way Winnie used to do.

As they came closer, I thought I was going to melt, right there on the spot. I couldn't believe my eyes. That young colt was the spitting image of his great grand dad.

Winnie ran near the fence and then stopped and began to buck, as though showing me how strong she had become. I clapped my hands, in approval and squealed at her. "Show me, baby. Show me!"

She hit a dead run and whizzed by me with such speed, my heart was racing with her. To my delight, her young colt was trying to keep up, his little tail whipping in the air. Then she trotted over to the fence, where we hugged and I cried. She talked, I talked, and it was a good time.

"This is a *good* place, Winnie. This is a *good* place. I'm so happy for you. I'm so glad to see you." Winnie tossed her head and slid down the fence to visit with Willie and her parents. Willie and I were drenched in tears and laughing.

My parting words to Winnie were, "You raise that boy to be just like you. You be my happy girl. Ok? I love you. I'm so happy for you. Bye, bye, baby".

We drove away while Willie and I stared out the back window, waving. It was an excruciatingly wonderful day.

About the Author: I live in southern Arizona, these days. The last I heard of Willie, she was living in NY.

While Winnie was a long ago story, I am forever remembering the wonderful excitement of those days. I can little understand why but my daughter and grandson, never tire of hearing the stories.

How I miss those times and constantly remind my children to cherish every moment. They will soon be gone.

www.ingramcontent.com/pod-product-compliance
Lightning Source LLC
Chambersburg PA
CBHW060642290526
45793CB00001B/367